WEALTH ADVENTURE

A guide to building a successful and wealthy life

Brian Andersen

Copyrighted © 2023 by

Brian Andersen

TABLE OF CONTENT

CHAPTER 1

INTRODUCTION

Preparing The Ground For Wealth

Understanding The Significance Of A Wealth Mindset

Setting Fiscal Goals

CHAPTER 2

BUILDING A SOLID FOUNDATION

Understanding Introductory Particular Finance Generalities

Areas Of Personal Finance

CHAPTER 3

INVESTING FOR GROWTH

Understanding The Power Of Compound Interest

How To Purchase Various Investments

CHAPTER 4

MAXIMIZING INCOME

Strategies For Earning More Money

Ideas For Passive Income

CHAPTER 5

GUARDING YOUR MONEY

Knowing The Significance Of Insurance

Planning Your Estate Can Help You Protect Your Assets

Lowering Taxes

Advice On How To Prepare For Retirement

CHAPTER 6

CONTINUING ON THE PATH

Retaining Your Motivation And Dedication To Your Wealth-Building Project

Examining And Modifying Your Financial Strategy

Coping With Setbacks And Unexpected Events

CHAPTER 7

CONCLUSION

The Significance Of Lifelong Learning And Development

12 Infinitely Valuable Items For A Wealthy Life

CHAPTER 1

INTRODUCTION

Wealth refers to the value of all the assets a person or household owns, minus all the liabilities they owe. Assets can include things like cash, investments, real estate, and personal property, while liabilities are debts and other financial obligations. The concept of wealth can be used to measure a person's financial well-being and can also be used to compare the financial status of different individuals or groups. There are many ways to accumulate wealth, such as through savings, investment, inheritance, or entrepreneurship. However, wealth inequality remains a major issue in many societies, with a small percentage of individuals or households owning a disproportionate amount of wealth compared to the rest of the population.

I'd like to go over the benefits of accumulating wealth in this part. I will go through the advantages of accumulating wealth for future generations as well as how having financial security may provide one flexibility and options in life. I'll also discuss the typical challenges people run into when attempting to accumulate wealth and how to get through them.

Preparing the ground for wealth creation

When it comes to increasing their money, everyone should have financial goals. Here's my opinion on how you may take charge of your wealth path.

Level 1: Financial stability

When you are confident in your financial status, you are said to be financially stable. If your finances are in order, there is nothing to worry about when it comes to paying your bills since you are confident in your financial situation. Financial security also entails being debt-free and having money set aside for future objectives. You also have enough cash on hand in this situation to handle unforeseen expenses.

When your current liquid assets are six times more than your monthly expenses, you are also considered financially stable. You have life and hospitalization insurance, so in the event that something were to happen to you, you could take care of yourself or your family's expenses. Financial stability is crucial since it protects you from experiencing financial stress and mental illnesses.

Level 2: Financial Security

When you have enough investments or other assets to pay for your essential costs on a passive basis, you are considered financially secure. Financial stability is defined as being debt-free and able to comfortably cover your monthly costs while still having money left over for savings. However, when you are financially stable, you don't need to worry about not having enough money for retirement or unexpected bills. Although anyone could accomplish it, relatively few people really succeed in doing so since achieving financial security is a difficult path. You need to have a comprehensive plan and work hard until you are financially secure. You can feel at ease knowing that your financial situation can meet your needs when you are no longer concerned about money.

Level 3: Financial Freedom

When you have enough assets with positive cash flows and passive income to support your existing standard of living, you are said to be financially free. Everyone is talking about how they've been financially liberated. They're not entirely off-base because financial independence will enable you to take charge of your finances and, more importantly, of your life. Living within your means and making sure that money is used for necessities like food, shelter, vacations, or recreation are key components of achieving financial freedom. Being wealthy or having a lot of money is not the point of this. It emphasizes the importance of having enough cash to cover your expenses instead. You may spend your valuable time doing the things you enjoy rather than working when you have enough residual income to support your living needs.

Level 4: Financial Abundance

When you get to this point, you have amassed enough assets with positive cash flows to produce enough passive income to support the lifestyle you want. It's all about having more than you need, as the name would imply. You don't have to worry about money to live a life of comfort and abundance.

Because you can afford to do what you love, this also implies that you can live your life in a way that feels real to you. This is the ultimate level of riches, allowing you to take delight in life's basic joys without being constrained by concern or stress about money. our opinion Nobody is perfect, and your journey is particular to you. One goal at a time, please. Setting financial Setting objectives for the future is a good place to start since, when you aren't working toward something specific, you tend to spend more than you should. To become financially secure, attempt to set your short-, mid-, and long-term financial goals early in life.

Understanding the significance of a wealth mindset

Still, you will see a pattern, and veritably many of them can attribute their success to one singularly amazing event if you look closely at the success stories of rich people. They'll say that their thinking is the main driver of their success. A wealth mindset is a combination of ideas, routines, and conduct that distinguishes rich people from the rest of the population. Making the most of the plutocracy you do have will be easier with a wealth mindset.

But it's not always simple. Spending less, making prudent investments, and seeking out low-threat strategies to enhance your fiscal position are all characteristics of a wealth mindset.

Setting fiscal goals

Setting SMART goals—specific, measurable, attainable, applicable, and time-bound is essential for success in numerous aspects of life, including accumulating wealth. This section will cover the value of setting fiscal objects as well as the procedures for doing so. We will also emphasize how pivotal it is to periodically examine and modify pretensions in light of evolving conditions. Do you want to produce a budget for a home in order to save up for a down payment? Have you thought about how to pay off your credit card and student loan debt? Alternatively, why not just make it a practice to pay your bills on time? Not sure where to begin or how to prioritize what you have already started? You may negotiate them with the help of this practical five-step approach.

1. Fantasize about your short- and long-term futures.

If you haven't thought about the kind of life you want now and in five years, you might think about how a plutocrat can help you realize your dreams—or if your plans change.

2. Classify fiscal pretensions as short-, medium-, or long-term.

Longer-term fiscal objectives might require further saving and, therefore, further planning. All told, we have fiscal objects that are six months to five years old. Mid-term fiscal objectives are defined as five to ten times out, while long-term fiscal objectives are defined as less than ten times out.

3. Set a target date for your fiscal intentions.

It helps to be unequivocal, even if the date changes over time. If your toddler will be attending council in 2035, you have a target date for your council savings. For your tenth marriage anniversary, would you like to visit all of Europe? You're apprehensive about the schedule you're aiming for. Target dates (PDF) should be added to your fiscal object spreadsheet.

4. Sort your financial ambitions according to their importance, need, or desire.

To help you decide which ideal to fund first, mark each one on your worksheet as critical, needed, or wanted. Consider the case when you have a "vital" short-term thing like adding your exigency fund. Still, trading in your impeccably performing auto is another short-term fiscal ideal; this is a "desire." You will know where to invest your plutocracy if it is tight for one month.

5. Estimate the current state of your savings.

You can add what you've previously saved after you know how important it is, what you want to save, and when each of your objects is due. Some objects might not call for current savings. That is fine; just get started right away.

For example, if you want to buy a house in two years and need $4,000 for a down payment, divide $3,000 by 24 months. So you know to put away $25 more each month to reach that ideal.

CHAPTER 2

BUILDING A SOLID FOUNDATION

Understanding introductory particular finance generalities

Budgeting, saving, and investing are just a few of the fundamentals of personal finance covered in this section. We'll also go over the basics of credit, including how it works, how to read and comprehend credit reports, and how to raise your credit score. The rest of the book will be built on this material.

The expression "particular finance" refers to managing your finances as well as saving and investing. It includes fiscal planning for withdrawals, levies, and estates, as well as banking, insurance, mortgages, and investments. The expression is constantly used to describe the entire sector that offers fiscal services to people and homes and provides them with fiscal and investment advice.

How you approach the forenamed matters is also told by your individual pretensions and wants, as well as a plan to meet those requirements within your means. Being financially smart is pivotal if you want to maximize your earnings and savings since it'll enable you to distinguish between good and bad advice and make wise fiscal choices.

Having a particular financial plan will help you achieve your fiscal objectives. These objects could be anything from having enough plutocrats to cover immediate charges to making withdrawal plans to putting down plutocrats for your child's council education. Your income, spending, saving, investing, and, in particular, safety, all go into this (insurance and estate planning).

Areas of Personal Finance

Income, saving, spending, investing, and protection are the five pillars of particular finance.

Income

The foundation of specific finance is income. The total amount of plutocracy you bring in that you can use for charges, savings, investments, and protection. Your income is made up of everything you earn. This covers pay, benefits, tips, and other forms of income.

Spending

Spending is a form of marketable outflow and constantly accounts for a large portion of income. Spending is anything a person uses their income to buy. Rent, mortgage, groceries, pastimes, eating out, home furnishings, house repairs, trips, and entertainment all fall under this category.

A vital element of personal finance is being able to control your expenditures. In order to avoid running out of money or getting into debt, people must make sure their expenditures are lower than their income. Financial ruin can result from debt, especially given the extravagant interest rates credit cards charge.

Saving

The capital that remains after spending goes into savings. Savings should be a thing for everyone to help with significant bills or extreme expenses. This calls for saving some capital, which can be challenging. No matter how tough it may be, everyone should endeavor to have at least some savings—between three and 12 months' worth of expenses—to cover any changes in income and have them retain or increase in value.

Investing

Investing entails buying means, generally stocks and bonds, in order to induce a return on the capital invested. The point of investing is to boost a person's wealth over and beyond their original investment. Since not all means increase in value and can witness a loss, investing does carry some trouble. For individuals who are unfamiliar with investing, it can be challenging. It's salutary to get a professional to help you with a marketable operation.

Protection

The term "protection" refers to the measures people take to guard their means against unlooked-for circumstances like conditions or accidents. Planning for your estate and withdrawal, as well as your life and health, are all forms of protection.

Personal Finance Services

Each of the five orders describes one or more financial planning services. Numerous companies presumably offer their guests these services to help them with budgeting and marketability. Among these services are:

Money Management, Debt, and Loans, Budgeting, Retirement, Assessments, Risk Administration, Estate Preparation, Investments, Insurance, Cards—Credit, Mortgage and covering, etc.

Particular Finance Strategies

It's wise to begin financial planning as soon as possible, but it's never too late to set financial goals for the freedom and security of your family. There is also some advice and prudent practices for handling specific finances.

Creating and adhering to a budget

Most people keep track of their monthly financial expenditures. A budget can give you a sense of financial control and make it simpler for you to save money for your goals. The trick is finding a financial mentoring system that works for you. You can make a budget with the help of the coming way.

Step 1 Calculate your net income

Your net income serves as the foundation of an effective budget. Your take-home pay is the sum of your income, lower-duty payments, and employer-sponsored benefits like withdrawal plans and health insurance. Fixing your attention on your gross pay rather than your net pay may drive you to overspend because you'll believe you have more marketable access than you actually do. Keep thorough records of your contracts and compensation if you're a freelancer, gig worker, contractor, or self-employed person to help manage erratic profits.

Step 2 Track your spending

Chancing out where your capital is going comes after determining how much you have coming in. You may find out what you are spending the most money on and where it would be easiest to cut costs by keeping track of and classifying your charges.

List your fixed charges first. These are typical monthly charges like AVS and machine payments, rent or mortgage payments, and so forth. Next, make a list of your variable charges, which include goods like groceries, gas, and entertainment that could differ from month to month. You might find openings to make savings in this region. Since credit card and bank statements constantly itemize or group your monthly charges, they are good places to start. Whatever is available, analogous to a pen and paper, a smartphone app, or online budgeting spreadsheets or templates, should be used to keep track of your quotidian spending.

Step 3: Establish reasonable expectations.

Make a list of your short- and long-term financial goals before you begin sorting through the data you've gathered. Short-term objects, which can be completed one to three times, might include goods like creating an emergency fund or reducing credit card debt. Long-term goals like withdrawal planning or funding your child's academy may take decades to negotiate. Although your pretensions don't have to be inflexible, knowing what they are can inspire you to stick to your spending plan. For example, if you know you're saving for a vacation, it might be simpler to reduce spending.

Step 4: Make a plan.

Where everything comes together is the distinction between what you actually spend and what you aspire to spend. To estimate your spending over the coming numerous months, use the list of variable and fixed charges that you have established. Also, make a distinction between your priorities and your net income. Consider establishing unambiguous, attainable spending caps for every expenditure order.

You could decide to prioritize your spending by dividing it into wants and needs. Gas, for example, is considered a necessity if you commute to work every day. Still, a monthly music subscription might be considered a want. This distinction becomes vital when you're trying to figure out how to reroute marketable toward your financial objectives.

Step 5: Acclimate your spending to stay on budget.

You can now make any needed variations so that you do not overspend and have enough plutocracy to go toward your pretensions after establishing your income and spending. The first place to make cuts should be toward your "wants." Can you watch a movie at home rather than go to the movies? If you've previously made adaptations to your spending on wants, pay particular attention to your yearly payment spending.

A "need" may, upon near examination, only be "hard to part with." Still, consider modifying your fixed charges. If your computations still do not make sense, for example, could you save further money by shopping around for a better deal on homeowners' or bus insurance? Large trade-offs are involved in similar choices, so precisely consider your options. Keep in mind that, indeed, modest savings can add up to a sizable sum. Making small adaptations over time can add up to a surprising number of redundant plutocrats.

Step 6: Review your budget regularly.

Once your budget is established, it's pivotal to regularly check it and your spending to make sure you're staying on track. There aren't many sure-fire effects on your budget. For example, your costs could change, you could get a raise, or you could achieve something and want to set new goals. Whatever the reason, establish the practice of routinely reviewing your budget by using the antedating procedures.

Erecting an exigency fund

A savings regard designated for unexpected requirements is an exigency fund. How to produce and manage an emergency fund.

1. Produce a budget

You can improve your understanding of how you spend your money by making a budget. When you do not know how you spend your money, you cannot start saving it.

Make a list of all of your yearly charges to start. Take stock for at least two months to determine which costs are necessary and voluntary. Once this is understood, you may start to organize your plutocracy, control your spending, and begin saving for emergencies.

2. Calculate your exigency fund thing

Calculate this by multiplying your total yearly essential charges by six, for illustration, if you are trying to accumulate an exigency fund to last for six months. Your exigency fund thing is the outgrowth.

3. Have an automatic deposit plan

Set up direct transfers from your source of income into your savings regard. Automating deposits makes saving simpler, guards against dereliction, and maintains progress toward your exigency fund thing.

4. Save unanticipated plutocrat

Save all unlooked-for income until you have attained your exigency fund target. A perk, a fiscal gift, a duty return, heritage, winning a bet, etc are all examples of unexpected income.

5. Continue saving after meeting your thing

An unforeseen expenditure can sometimes exceed a six-month exigency reserve because life happens. In that case, you will be pleased to have more in your exigency fund if you've been unemployed for more than six months.

Effects to know once you have your emergency fund

What do you do now that you have an exigency fund set up? Assume you can't take it anymore. Would you allow the plutocrats in your savings account to deteriorate due to affectation?

Availability

The plutocrat must be available at all times. Keep your cash close by so you can get it quickly. You may need to respond to situations right away and cannot stay for a delicate pullout process.

Separate investment fund from exigency fund

Make a clear distinction between urgency and financial investment. This makes sure that you know exactly what to put where.

Where to Keep Your Emergency Fund

Then, now that you're concerned about the considerations, there are several places you can secure your emergency fund.

1. High-yield savings regard

This is the ideal time to save your emergency fund. Find banks (or online banks) that give simple access and pay a reasonable yield.

2. Savings regard with reach- in installation

A reach-in installation makes sure that finances that exceed a destined threshold are transferred to a fixed deposit that you can pierce when you need cash. Your fund could make further gains in this situation than a typical savings account.

3. Short-term fixed deposits

Still, you can also arrange a short-term fixed deposit with your bank, if you want to keep from using the plutocracy for your savings. Before opening them, just be sure you understand the terms and conditions.

4. Liquid collective finances

Term bills, instruments of deposit, and other short-term fixed-income instruments are all investments made by liquid collective finances. They're more liquid and offer a slightly lower return than fixed deposits.

Tip: There are distinct regulations for each of these choices. It's better to divide your emergency savings among them as you see fit rather than keeping them entirely in one position.

Bottom Line

An emergency fund is the most effective way to save for unexpected disasters and avoid making poor financial decisions in times of need.

Whether you're ready for them or not, extremities can come. But at Leadway, our savings plans make sure that the plutocrat will be there for you if they do. Debt can make it difficult to pay off debt and build wealth. The colorful debts and their advantages and disadvantages will be covered in this section. We'll also talk about how to avoid accumulating debt while pregnant as well as quick and effective debt repayment strategies.

Still, cut your borrowing costs, or just reduce your debt, if you want to qualify for new credit. Then there are some tactics to consider while looking at prepayment options that can speed up your debt repayment.

Tips for paying off debt

Pay further than the minimal

Paying more than the minimum each month will help you pay off your debt and reduce your interest costs. The secret to paying off your loan more quickly is to constantly make redundant payments. Some lenders permit you to make a fresh payment each month, with the caveat that all fresh payments must be applied to the account. Before you begin, review the terms of your loan to see if there are any new costs or repayment penalties.

Pay further than formerly a month

Once a month, pay off more than the minimum on your credit card bills. This can make it simpler for you to keep track of how much debt you have. Regularly paying your credit card statement may also help reduce your balance to the available credit rate. The percentage of your total available credit that's presently being used is known as your credit operation rate. One of the factors credit reporting companies take into account when determining your credit score is the application rate.

Pay off your most precious loan first

The loan with the highest interest rate is the one that will bring you the most money. By paying it off first, you lower your overall debt and the total amount of interest you pay. Also, to reduce your overall cost, keep paying off the debts with the highest interest rates. This fashion of debt prepayment is also known as the "avalanche approach."

Consider the snowball system of paying off debts

In order to do this, you must start with your lowest balance, pay it off, and also apply the same payment to the next-lowest balance as you progress to the topmost balance. As each quantum is paid off, using this fashion can help you gain instigation. Review the Snowball versus Avalanche debt prepayment strategies to comprehend the benefits and downsides of this debt reduction plan.

Keep track of bills and pay them at cheaper times. Use bill reminders and online bill payments to stay on top of your debt. Simply plan out the quantities and due dates for your payments. You can also create payment monuments and sign up to receive eBills from payees who support electronic invoicing.

CHAPTER 3

INVESTING FOR GROWTH

Understanding the power of compound interest

The interest on a loan or deposit that is calculated using both the initial principal and the accrued interest from prior periods is known as compound interest. We'll talk about how compound interest works, its strength over time, and how you can take advantage of it.

What Is Growth Investing?

Growing an investor's capital is the main goal of the investment style and technique known as "growth investing." Growth stocks, or young or tiny businesses whose earnings are anticipated to increase at an above-average rate compared to their industry sector or the broader market, are the type of securities that growth investors typically invest in.

Many investors find growth investing to be very appealing since purchasing shares in emerging firms can result in substantial returns (as long as the companies are successful). But because they haven't been tested, these businesses frequently carry a high level of risk. Value investment and growth investment can be compared. Choosing stocks that appear to be trading for less than their intrinsic or book worth is part of the value investing technique.

Understanding Growth Investing

Growth investors often seek investments in fast-developing areas (or even entire industries) that are home to emerging products and services. Growth investors seek gains through capital appreciation, or the gains they will realize when they sell their shares (as opposed to dividends they receive while they own them). In reality, rather than providing dividends to their shareholders, the majority of growth-stock companies reinvest their profits back into the company.

These businesses typically have great promise but are small and young. They can also be new public corporations that have recently begun trading. The underlying assumption is that as the business grows and prospers, better earnings or revenues will ultimately result in higher stock values. Therefore, growth stocks may trade with a high price-to-earnings (P/E) ratio. They might not be earning money right now, but they should in the future. This is due to the possibility that they possess patents or have access to technologies that provide them with an advantage over rivals in their field.

They reinvest the money to create even more cutting-edge technology in order to stay one step ahead of rivals, and they pursue patents to guarantee longer-term growth. Growth investing is also referred to as a "capital growth strategy" or a "capital appreciation strategy," since investors want to maximize their capital profits.

Evaluating a Company's Potential for Growth

The growth potential of a business or market is examined by growth investors. It takes some degree of human interpretation, based on objective and subjective elements, as well as personal judgment, to assess this potential because there is no definitive method for doing so. Growth investors may use specific criteria or procedures as a foundation for their study, but these approaches must be used with consideration for the unique circumstances of each company: more specifically, how it currently compares to its previous financial and industry performance.

Strong Forward Earnings Growth

An earnings announcement is a formal, public declaration of a company's financial success for a given timeframe, usually a quarter or a year. During earnings season, these announcements are made on certain days and preceded by earnings projections provided by equity analysts. These projections are what growth investors focus on when trying to identify which businesses are most likely to develop faster than the industry as a whole.

Strong Profit Margins

The pretax profit margin is determined by subtracting all costs (other than taxes) from sales and dividing by sales. It's a crucial indicator to take into account because a business may see tremendous sales growth but weak profitability growth, which may be a sign that management is not effectively managing costs and revenues. In general, a company may be a good growth prospect if its pretax profit margins are higher than those of its industry and its previous five-year average.

Strong Return on Equity(ROE)

The pretax profit margin is determined by eliminating all costs (other than levies) from deals and dividing them by deals. It's a pivotal index to take into account because a business may see tremendous deal growth but weak profitability growth, which may be a sign that the operation isn't effectively managing costs and earnings. In general, a company may be a good growth prospect if its pretax profit perimeters are more advanced than those of its assiduity and its former five-time normal.

Different types of investments and their implicit returns

Numerous people find investing intimidating because there are so many possibilities, and it can be grueling to choose which investments are best for your account. This composition describes ten of the most popular investing orders, from equities to goods, and discusses why you would wish to include each one in your portfolio. If you are serious about investing, hiring a financial advisor who can guide you and help you choose which investments will help you achieve your goals may make sense.

1. Stocks

The most well-known and straightforward kind of investing is likely to be in stocks, generally referred to as shares or equities. Purchasing stock entitles you to power in an intimately listed pot. You may buy stock in numerous of the largest companies in the nation since they're intimately listed. Among the many examples are Microsoft, Apple, and Exxon. How to induce income When you buy a stock, you hope the price will rise so that you can sell it later and become a plutocrat. Of course, there's a chance that the stock's price could drop, in which case you would lose money.

2. Bonds

In substance, you're advancing a plutocrat to an association when you buy a bond. Generally, this would be a company or a government agency. Original governments issue external bonds, whereas businesses issue commercial bonds. Investors can buy Treasury bonds, notes, and bills, which are all debt securities issued by the US Treasury.

How to induce income Interest payments are made to the investor or lender while the plutocrat is being espoused. You get your investment back when the bond matures, which means you've held it for the time period specified in the contract. Bonds typically have a lower rate of return than stocks, but they also frequently carry lower threats. Of course, there's still some peril involved. Both the government and the reality from which you buy the bond are subject to failure. But Treasury bonds, notes, and bills are regarded as veritably secure means.

3. Collective finances

A collective fund is a collection of multitudinous investors' plutocracy that's astronomically invested in a variety of businesses. Both laboriously and passively managed collective finances are available. A fund director who chooses which securities to invest in runs a laboriously managed fund. By opting for investments that will outperform such an indicator, fund directors constantly strive to beat the standard request indicator. An indicator fund, generally referred to as an "unresistant operation," simply follows a significant stock request indicator like the Dow Jones Industrial Average or the S&P 500. Collective finances have access to a wide range of instruments, including derivatives, stocks, bonds, goods, and currencies.

Depending on the means they're invested in, collective finances might have numerous of the same pitfalls as stocks and bonds. Still, because the means are naturally diversified, the threat is constantly lower.

How to induce income When the value of the stocks, bonds, and other packaged securities that the collective fund invests in increases, investors profit from the collective fund. The managing company and reduction brokerages both offer direct purchasing options for them. However, keep in mind that there is a constant minimum investment as well as a periodic charge.

4. Exchange- Traded funds (ETFs)

Collective finances and exchange-traded funds (ETFs) both correspond to a group of investments that follow a request indicator. Shares in ETFs are bought and sold on the stock exchange, as opposed to collective finances, which must be bought through a fund provider. While the value of collective finances is simply the net asset value of your investments, which is determined at the conclusion of each trading session, their price changes throughout the trading day.

How to induce income ETFs to induce profit by pooling the returns from all of their investments. Because they're more diversified than individual stocks, ETFs are constantly suggested to neophyte investors. By opting for an ETF that follows a broad indicator, you can indeed reduce the threat. Analogous to collective finances, you can benefit from an ETF by dealing with it as its value increases.

5. Instruments of Deposit (CDs)

Investment experts view certificates of deposit (CDs) as veritably low-threat options. You advance a plutocrat to a bank for a fixed period of time, and you get interested in that plutocrat. You admit your investment back on with the destined quantum of interest after that time period has passed. Your interest rate is presumably going to be advanced the longer the loan term. The implicit return is low, but the peril is also low.

How to benefit With a CD, you profit from the interest you earn throughout the course of the deposit. For long-term fiscal savings, CDs are a solid choice. They're FDIC- insured up to $,000, which would cover your finances indeed if your bank were to fail, so there are no significant troubles. nonetheless, you must be certain that you will not bear the finances during the CD's term because early recessions are subject to severe penalties.

6. Pension Programs

A retirement plan is an investment account where participants deposit funds for retirement and that has special tax advantages. There are many different types of retirement plans, including workplace retirement plans provided by your employer like 401(k) and 403(b) plans. You might be eligible to start an individual retirement account (IRA) or a Roth IRA if your employer does not provide a retirement plan.

How to bring in money: Retirement plans are not a separate class of investments in and of themselves but rather a vehicle to purchase stocks, bonds, and funds in two tax-advantaged ways. You may invest pretax money in the first one (as with a traditional IRA). You can withdraw money from the second one without having to pay taxes on it. The investments carry the same risks as if you had bought them separately from a retirement plan.

7. Choices

An option is a slightly more complex or involved way to buy stock. When you buy an option, you gain the right to buy or sell an asset at a particular price and moment. There are two types of options: call options, which are used to sell options, and put options, which are used to buy assets.

How to bring in money: As an investor, you set a stock's price with the hope that its value will rise. The risk associated with an option is that the stock can also lose money. If the stock price decreases from the time you first bought it, you forfeit the money from the contract. Options trading involves advanced financial techniques, so novice investors should use caution.

8. Pensions

An insurance policy and recurring payments are exchanged when you buy an annuity. Although they sometimes begin years in advance, these payments typically begin when you reach retirement. As a result, many people incorporate annuities into their retirement savings plans.

Annuities come in many different forms. They might be around forever or simply for a short while. They can demand a one-time payment in advance or regular premium payments. They might be merely insurance policies with no relation to the markets, or they might be loosely related to the stock market. Payments may be made immediately or deferred until a specific day and time. They might be both stable and flexible.

How to get paid: An additional source of retirement income may be guaranteed by annuities. They don't have high growth, but they do have a minimal risk level. Investors typically view them as advantageous supplements to their retirement funds rather than their main source of income.

Derivatives, 9.

A "derivative" financial product derives its value from another asset. It is a two-party agreement resembling an annuity. But in this situation, the contract is a promise to sell something at a specific price in the future. By choosing to purchase the derivative, the investor is making a bet that the value won't decrease. Derivatives are typically purchased by institutional investors since they are viewed as more complex assets.

The following are the top three categories of derivatives:

Options agreements: The ability to buy or sell a specific asset at a specific price at a specific time in the future is provided by an option. With a put option, you can sell the asset at that price, or with a call option, you can buy it at that price.

Future sales agreements: A future contract ensures that a sale will occur at the designated hour on the designated day. Swaps are agreements between two parties to trade future cash flows.

How to get paid: Investing in derivatives can be rewarding if you anticipate price changes correctly. If, for example, you commit to purchasing copper for $1,000 in nine months but the market price is $2,000 at that time, your investment has practically quadrupled.

How to Purchase Various Investments

There are two methods by which you might purchase the various assets you might be interested in, but in both situations, you'll need to have an active investment account. Both are straightforward to carry out, but only one provides a service that is completely complete for you. The following are the two primary methods for getting the types of investments you want:

Create a Brokerage Account Online: You can create a brokerage account online to get going right away because you can buy stocks, bonds, mutual funds, and more in a matter of minutes. The only negative aspect is that you will be responsible for all financial decisions.

Hire a Financial Advisor: Another choice for buying different investment types is to hire a financial advisor. In addition to offering you access to purchase and trade assets, the adviser can assist you in creating a thorough financial plan and successfully preparing for retirement. This process is more automated because you only need to approve trades or investments; the advisor takes care of the intricacies. Your advisor can assist you with opening a brokerage account if necessary.

The conclusion

Several different investments can be made. While some are suitable for beginners, others require more research and education. Whatever your goal may be, you have a few respectable options because each type of investment has a distinct level of risk and reward. Investors should take each sort of investment before selecting an asset allocation that is consistent with their overall financial objectives.

CHAPTER 4

MAXIMIZING INCOME

Strategies for earning more money

You'll need to earn your money the hard way—by working for it—unless you're fortunate enough to have been born into a spendthrift trust fund. However, having a financial understanding can help you. Try these four simple methods for making money, and one of them might help you amass a fortune.

Selling Your Time

When it comes to making money, this is the source that most individuals consider. This is the payment you make to an employer in exchange for giving them your time; it's frequently referred to as a salary or wage. Parents with good intentions frequently advise their kids to choose a "good career," preferably one with benefits.

Your hourly pay will depend on how uncommon and in-demand your skills are. Given the scarcity of qualified candidates, a skilled brain surgeon, for example, can earn millions of dollars annually.

A person who pushes carts for a bargain retailer makes less money, not because they are any less useful as people, but rather because there is a large pool of available labor, which drives down wages.

You must work more, put more effort into improving your rate, or do a combination of the two in order to increase your income. Because you only make money while you're actually working, this type of income is the most active way to make a living. If you enjoy your job, working nonstop to get money could be acceptable, but for many people, there might be other things they'd rather do more of.

Earn interest on money lent

You receive this kind of income from borrowers who pay you to "rent" your capital. You'll hear the word "capital" used frequently on Wall Street to refer to funds you've set aside for investments.

For instance, you are lending money to the bank when you purchase a certificate of deposit (CD) at a bank in exchange for a fixed rate of return. The bank "rents" the money from you and then lends it out at a higher interest rate, keeping the difference for itself.

Side Hustle Tips for the New Year

It's crucial to pick a side business that matches your personality and skill set; for example, if you hate selling, you probably shouldn't launch a venture that requires you to interact with customers one-on-one. A pet service, however, would be an excellent fit if you have a lot of experience with animals. Ensure that you are spending your time on the tasks that are most important.

Six professionals, all of whom have launched side enterprises and assisted others in creating their own successful side businesses, were consulted for advice.

1. Start small, and don't invest right away

One cannot overestimate the importance of starting small. You will be miles ahead of those who start tomorrow if you take baby steps today to establish a side business.

By starting small, you may also allocate your resources in an effective manner. The most terrifying error people make is attempting to have everything perfect before receiving any genuine validation. Don't spend $30,000, or even $3,000, on a website before you get just one client. Then, if you have traction and want to invest, go for it. Validate it and sell it first.

It's considerably less dangerous to gradually expand your side business because it allows you to make changes along the way.

2. Select the ideal side business for yourself

The ideal side gig for you should satisfy three requirements: you should enjoy it, be competent at it, and be able to make money at it. Although achieving this objective may seem difficult, you can begin by simply focusing on your strengths. We consider what we already know to be unimportant and take it for granted. But a new firm cannot be built on the strength of just one ability.

Consider consulting individuals who are most familiar to you if you are having problems identifying your strongest skills. Ask your friends, family, or coworkers to identify your strengths for you. You could also consider your prior expertise. What is a question that individuals always ask you? For us, it was debt repayment, so we created an online course on the subject.

Accept the abilities you've developed at your present or past work, as they may be useful for a side business. You can go out and make your own thing on the side and get paid for it as long as there is no conflict with your existing work. A teacher can provide online tutoring. If you work as a mechanic, you can also repair and resell used vehicles. Why not use your skills to generate income for yourself instead of just your employer?

Your side business should be enjoyable for you and add value to your life, not take away from it. However, don't set the standard so high that nothing will ever be able to achieve it. You must enjoy it. It doesn't have to be a lifelong interest because you can look for that for a lifetime. Because there are always challenges in business, you need to appreciate what you're doing.

Insert yourself where the money is already flowing if you're wondering how to generate money with a side hustle. Instead of opening your own internet store in the beginning, sell your physical goods where consumers already shop, such as on eBay, Etsy, and Amazon.

Consider: "How are customers resolving this issue already?" If you can integrate into those marketplaces and make it simple for clients to do business with you, you're positioning yourself for success.

3. Be clear about your reasons for starting

Not everyone wants to quit their full-time position. Your motivation can be to pay off debt, accumulate an emergency fund, increase your retirement investment, or save money for a down payment on a home.

It is much easier to keep track of your progress when you start with the end in mind. Remember that your side venture doesn't have to take off and become the next great thing. Even if it doesn't directly help you achieve your goals, it still might be a success.

4. Set time priorities.

The 24/7 "rise and grind" attitude holds that in order to build a successful side business, you must forego sleep, among other things. If you still think you won't have enough time to finish a task right now. Once you're on the go, you find that opportunities are easier to see. The little time you do have is crucial since you will never have a 38-hour block of time to do a project.

5. Demand the amount you're worth.

When you're afraid to charge people for your services, it can be quite tough to get past your first side gig. When I started, I was hesitant. Should I actually charge for promotions? But as time went on, I realized that I was really only filling a need for another company.

Even though the majority of people are really wary about it, you must have a very clear method of payment and charge for your services. And it's essential to commit a sizeable percentage of your time to activities that actually generate income. You can spend a lot of time doing busy work that is useless. You should plan to devote 80% of your time to client acquisition in the first few months.

6. Keep your integrity and professionalism.

Negotiating a pay raise can be difficult if you don't know what success looks like for you. Do you wish to advance? I can tell you that this will work as soon as you leave your emotions at the door.

Please keep in mind that first impressions count, so you must always come across as sincere and professional. Avoid the temptation to demand a pay raise through threats of coercion. Instead, you should take a deliberate approach. Being arrogant or frightening is sometimes ineffective. Steer clear of being arrogant, ungrateful, or disparaging to others. The most crucial thing is to refrain from evaluating yourself against your coworkers. No matter what happens, keep your cool. Stressing yourself out won't get you the raise you want.

7. Before submitting your presentation, review it.

You must remain confident and prepared to deliver the presentation if the goal is to persuade your boss that you merit a raise. Because of this, you ought to practice speaking with your supervisor face-to-face.

If your boss asks for further information, consider having various responses ready. This is especially beneficial if you experience resistance or a flat-out "no." To gain a sense of the challenges or questions the manager can pose, think about practicing with a family member or acquaintance.

8. Make time to speak with your manager about this.

This tactic is effective because it demonstrates to your manager that you are a well-organized individual. You have time to prepare for D-Day by scheduling a conversation regarding your pay raise. The best time to do this is preferably just after a financially successful quarter. On the other hand, you can choose to do it at a suitable period of the year or during a scheduled performance review.

Choose a time for your meeting that will help you ensure that your employer is fully present. Avoid approaching your boss's office in the same way that other individuals do to start a pay negotiation.

9. Don't quote the wage right away.

Rushing to share your salary could send the wrong message to your manager. Exercise caution when discussing money issues with your boss. It is suggested that you enter the meeting to discuss the specifics after your supervisor has revealed the compensation rate.

You are free to request a few extra days to think over the offer. When your supervisor gives you some wiggle room, you can evaluate the circumstances and choose the course of action that will best meet your needs. By looking, you can assess if there is still room to negotiate a better rate or to extend your terms.

On the other hand, if your boss accepts your demands right away, consider the possibility that you started out too slowly. That is partially understandable because you might think that by bringing up a higher quote, you are upsetting your boss. Additionally, it makes clear why your boss should make the first move rather than you.

10. Make a list of your justifications for the rise.

Think beyond the box when negotiating your wage and stress the importance of a higher salary to your overall production. This can take the form of a flexible schedule, more training, a bigger role with more responsibility, working from home, or even more vacation time. Before selecting what you're willing to accept, make sure you've established what you think is necessary.

11. Display your performance history.

Your boss has a right to be aware of the justifications for granting your request. Show them some evidence; in this scenario, your performance history is perhaps the greatest source. By doing this, you can show your boss that you are more forthcoming with him. If you have a history of outstanding achievement, you can be guaranteed that you will have the upper hand in the negotiation.

You can choose to use a performance plan that lists all of your successes. By doing this, you will show the company how much it may cost to replace you while also showcasing your worth.

For instance, you might decide to discuss with your employer the goals you two set together and what you've done so far to attain them. Believe me, it functions perfectly. I have applied for a wage raise several times when I felt I needed one to reflect my worth.

12. Do some paid research to support your request.

You are in a stronger position because your research on average salaries shows that you have a good case for asking for a wage increase. This knowledge is useful since it will give you leverage when the conversation starts. Instead, you may look for jobs in a similar field on well-known job forums and compare the income to what you are currently making. To build your connections, you may also consider concentrating on professions that are comparable in your neighborhood. Upwork, Simply Hired, Payscale and Glassdoor are all helpful websites.

13. Think about how the rise would increase your productivity.

It's true that you should focus your conversations on how the pay increase will increase your productivity. Instead of viewing your employer and the conversations as a conflict between you two, think of them as a team. You can rapidly let go of the tension and find serenity by doing this.

You must be knowledgeable about the matter at hand. As a result, during the conversation, you should project confidence and maintain eye contact. Your body language and the things you say to your manager during the conversations are very crucial. Be prepared to put in the time and effort required to achieve your goal if, as I do, you feel that you deserve a salary raise. Everything is subject to how you are feeling. Your perspective is crucial in these situations.

It's time for you to shine. The fundraising will now proceed.

Ideas for passive income

The first step in developing a consistent income stream is choosing the passive source of income that makes the most sense for you. Whether you want to start a business or make a financial investment, here are nine ideas to consider for your passive income strategy:

1. Put money into investments.

Buying stocks, bonds, mutual funds, and peer-to-peer lending are just a few examples of financial investments; they require little follow-up work while interest is accruing. Consult a financial advisor to help you choose the investments that are best for you.

2. Have a rental home.

Whether you rent to long-term or transient renters, rental revenue can be a dependable source of additional money, but it still necessitates all the usual upkeep on the property.

3. Open up a print-on-demand business.

You can sell your original designs for t-shirts, caps, mugs, posters, and other products by opening a print-on-demand store without having to worry about inventory or fulfillment. It only takes a few steps to get started: choose your supplier (such as Printful, Printify, or Gelato), submit your file, choose the products you want to sell, and promote them on your website.

4. Self-publication

If you have a lot of expertise or a brilliant story idea, you can write a book and sell it online. Many individuals use a service like Kindle Direct Publishing, which enables you to turn your writing into an ebook or print copy and sell it on Amazon.

5. Market workbooks.

You can buy online worksheets and upload them to many places. This is often done by creating a worksheet that is printable and publishing it to a website like Etsy or Teachers Pay Teachers, where users may pay to download and use your work.

6. Make template sales.

If you enjoy creating digital organization systems in programs like Microsoft Excel or Notion, you might be able to earn money from your templates. Many people sell their creations on Etsy and other online marketplaces.

7. Produce material.

By uploading your original works to YouTube and setting up your account for monetization through the YouTube Partner Program, you can earn money if you prefer utilizing video as your medium. There are some requirements to join the YouTube Partner Program, such as having a particular number of subscribers and views. You can make any type of video you wish, though, including instructive, short films, ones with original music, and even ones with ambient noise.

8. Design a web-based course.

Between publishing a book, selling worksheets and templates, and producing content, you can decide to package your resources as an online course. Many people create their content using programs like Teachable or Thinkific before hosting their courses on their own websites.

9. Market stock images.

Whether you're a beginner or an expert photographer, you may sell your original photos as stock images on websites like Alamy, Shutterstock, Stocksy, or Adobe Stock. Developers can generate a passive income by creating mobile software and reselling it on the Apple App Store or Google Play.

CHAPTER 5

GUARDING YOUR MONEY

Knowing the significance of insurance

There is no question that you would feel better at ease knowing that you and your loved ones are financially secure against a range of unforeseen scenarios. A terrible death or a medical emergency might happen at any time, among other life uncertainties. A collision or damage to your automobile, property, etc. is also included in this category.

You could run out of money if you have to cope with the financial consequences of these scenarios. You might need to draw on part of your or your family's funds. To effectively protect yourself and your family from risks to your life, health, and property, you and your family desperately need insurance.

Required Insurance

Insurance plans may be useful for anybody wanting to protect their family, property, and selves from financial danger or losses. Insurance plans will help with future medical expenses, hospital stays, catching any illnesses, and treatment. Insurance coverage can help a family make up for financial losses brought on by the premature death of their main source of income. The insured person's family can also settle any obligations that have accrued over the course of the insured person's lifetime, such as house loans or other debts.

Insurance protection will help your family keep their standard of living if you die away in the future. This will let them use the one-time insurance benefit to cover household bills. The insurance money will also cover all expenses in the event of the policyholder's death, accident, or medical emergency, allowing your family to breathe easier.

Making insurance plans will help you protect your child's future academic prospects. They will make sure that your kids have enough money to live comfortably while following their ambitions and passions without giving anything up, even while you are not around.

In addition to basic protection, many insurance contracts include investment and savings options. These support monetary savings and wealth accumulation through regular investments. Depending on your future needs and objectives, you regularly pay premiums, with a share going toward life insurance and the other into either a savings or investment plan.

Insurance may assist in securing your home in the case of any unforeseen calamity or catastrophe. Your house insurance policy will help you acquire coverage for property damage and, if necessary, cover the cost of repairs or rebuilding. If your house and assets are covered by insurance, you can use the money to purchase replacement goods.

Aids with long-term objectives

One of the most important benefits of life insurance is the capacity to save and grow capital. Among other things, you can use this money to save for your child's education or wedding, buy a home, start a company, or other long-term goals.

Useful for planning retirement

By getting life insurance, you may keep your financial freedom even after you retire. You receive a set income for the remainder of your days through life insurance and annuity plans. They are low-risk strategies that help you maintain your current standard of living, pay for medical expenses, and accomplish your post-retirement goals.

Planning your estate can help you protect your assets.

Making a will is a crucial part of estate planning because it serves as a form of legally enforceable agreement that outlines your preferences for what should happen after your passing, including who should handle your estate administration and how your assets should be dispersed. Additionally, a will might include instructions on how to care for any dependents or pets you may have. Without a will, a probate court could administer your estate, which might lead to someone other than the beneficiaries receiving your assets. If you don't create a will, your loved ones could have to wait longer for your estate to be resolved.

#1: Tell Your Loved Ones

Ahead of time, communicating with your loved ones on what to anticipate from your estate after your demise does not guarantee that your preferences would be honored. Without correctly designating people and things, there is a high likelihood that your plans won't be carried out. To prevent these problems and ensure that your assets are passed on to the people you want, you should name beneficiaries for all of your assets and routinely check accounts to make sure that your preferences remain appropriate.

#2: Use Transfer on Death Deeds as an Option

Transfer on death deeds are utilized in the state of New York to distribute assets to surviving family members. Without the need for probate, these documents make it possible to transfer ownership of assets to a grantee-beneficiary.

#3: Think About Designating A Trustee

Many individuals worry about what will happen to the belongings of their loved ones once they pass away. Some individuals worry about relatives they believe may not be excellent with money. Trust is one of the best ways to protect your belongings. You can select a trustee who will distribute your assets according to their judgment, and assets held in a trust are not subject to estate taxes. Remember that once you transfer property into a trust, you are no longer considered the owner of that property. Making a trust may be difficult, especially when there are several assets at stake.

Number 4: Gift Assets

If your assets are subject to heavy taxes that might leave your loved ones with less than you would have expected, you should think about gifting them assets while you are still alive. A person is now free from taxes in the US if they give one individual up to $15,000 per year. If you plan to give assets in this way, don't forget to account for asset appreciation. Depending on when you pass the gift on, your loved ones may be required to pay the value if the gift is altered after your death and exceeds the $15,000 tax threshold.

Lowering taxes

Make a retirement account contribution

One of the easiest and most generally applicable methods to reduce taxable income is to make contributions to retirement plans. Your taxable income can be reduced by traditional 401(k) and IRA contributions, which decrease the amount of federal tax you owe. These accounts likewise grow tax-free up until retirement. There are Roth accounts that are financed using previously taxed funds. Even if you don't receive a tax deduction, the money in the account grows tax-free and can be taken tax-free in retirement.

Contributions to employer 401(k) accounts must be made by the end of the calendar year, while tax-deductible contributions to ordinary IRAs can be made up to the April 18 tax filing deadline.

Establish a Health Savings Account

If you have a high-deductible medical plan that is eligible, contributing to a health savings account is another way to lower your taxable income. It won't be taxed if you spend the money on medical costs. These accounts permit tax-free withdrawals for qualified medical expenses, tax-deferred growth, and immediate tax deductions on donations. Any amount that is left over at the end of the year can be carried over forever, just like the assets in a retirement plan.

At work, look for flexible spending accounts.

Even if you don't have a high-deductible health insurance plan, you can still use tax-free money from your flexible spending account at work to pay for medical expenses.

Making retirement plans

Eventually, you would have to say goodbye to your 9-5 obligations and drop off your work bag for the final time. This major shift in your daily routine is referred to as "retirement." Planning for retirement requires work and, of course, money because it is not a simple process.

Advice on How to Prepare for Retirement

When to Begin Planning

When should you start establishing retirement plans? Now, in three words, describe yourself in your twenties. The more time you allow your money to develop through planning, the better. Even if you haven't given retirement any thought, don't think that your career is over. It's never too late to start saving money in local and foreign currencies because their worth will rise over time. You could avoid having to play catch-up for too long by making wise investments.

Identify your retirement spending requirements

Most respondents predict that they will only spend between 70% and 80% of what they spent annually before retirement. This kind of presumption is usually proven to be false, especially when unplanned medical expenses pop up. By establishing reasonable assumptions about your spending habits after retirement, you may estimate the required amount for your retirement portfolio. Many retirees spend their first several years of retirement traveling extensively or buying the house, car, or apparel of their dreams. Contrary to popular belief, ensure that your post-retirement spending practices and expectations are reasonable.

Set Your Financial Objectives in Order

Having goals does not end when you reach retirement. Building a house, moving overseas, launching a small business, and making other investments are a few of these goals. When developing retirement plans, remember to take your objectives into consideration.

CHAPTER 6

CONTINUING ON THE PATH

Retaining your Motivation and Dedication to your Wealth-building Project

It might be difficult to maintain motivation even if the highs and lows of achieving your goals are normal—even anticipated. Here are some ideas to help you or others who are struggling with financial motivation.

1. Understand your "why"

You may have heard that building credit and conserving money are smart decisions. However, if you don't know why you have to perform these things, to enjoy retirement free from financial worries. Whatever your "why" may be, it may keep you motivated and on task.

2. Make smart goals

It is much simpler to stay motivated when you are working toward a goal. Your financial decisions may be influenced by your objectives, which act as your "why." Whether these goals are short-term or long-term, it's a good idea to apply the S.M.A.R.T. (Specific, Measurable, Achievable, Relevant, Time-bound) goal-setting method. If you're having trouble coming up with a decent goal, check out these financial goals from actual college students to get your creative juices flowing.

3. Keep visible cues about your objective (s)

Once you've decided what you want to achieve, keeping track of your progress is easy. Make a goal thermometer or spreadsheet and stick it to your refrigerator or mirror so you can see it every day. When you visualize your goals, you have a daily reminder of what you're trying to achieve. Saying no to expensive social occasions or hasty purchases of new clothes or shoes may enable you to see the bigger picture.

4. Deconstruct bigger objectives

Longer-term goals, such as setting up an emergency fund, may seem intimidating, even if you take all the necessary steps and develop a goal you're driven to fulfill. To avoid long-term despair, split those goals into more achievable stages. You should save three to six months' worth of expenses for emergencies.

Until you reach or surpass it, you can divide this goal's achievement into one-month milestones. A one-month emergency fund may be saved far more easily than a six-month or longer emergency reserve. Your finances will stay on track, and your financial outlook will improve if you accomplish a lot of little goals that add up to a bigger one.

5. Honor victories (big or small)

As you begin to achieve your larger goals after breaking them down, don't forget to rejoice. Every time you accomplish one of your goals on your financial path, you must give yourself a small reward. If your goal is to raise your credit score above 700, you should get dessert at your favorite ice cream parlor. Paying off your debt is another financial achievement worth celebrating. You may purchase a bike, an easel, or something else as a prize for your accomplishment. Participating in these modest activities will help you stay motivated, but watch your spending.

6. Surround yourself with supportive individuals

If your friends and family regularly put you in difficult financial positions, it may start to wear on you. As soon as it is practical, surround yourself with individuals who will help you manage your funds. These motivating people will push you to succeed rather than hold you back. Even better, as you navigate your separate financial journeys, you can support one another.

7. Increase your financial knowledge

There is always more to learn, even if you believe you understand money and all that goes with it. Reading books or blogs on investing and saving techniques can help you develop a more well-rounded financial outlook, but you don't have to be a reader to improve your financial literacy. Instead, you could enjoy listening to financial podcasts or watching instructional videos online.

As you learn more, you may want to invest in a different retirement plan or create a larger emergency fund. Your ambitions will undoubtedly change as you learn more about the financial world.

8. Continue the forward motion

You won't always be excited and inspired since progress doesn't always have to be linear. If you run across obstacles along the road, that's okay. As long as you don't take any substantial steps backward, you are still getting closer to your goal of having a stable financial future. The greatest thing you can do is keep your attention on the subject at hand and proceed. As soon as you reach your financial goal, your zeal and drive will return.

You could have a better notion of how to keep your excitement for your money along the trip after reading these recommendations. These tips will make it easier for you to take responsibility for your financial decisions and handle your financial achievements and disappointments.

Remember that even if you maxed out your credit cards, made poor purchases of products and services, or just hit rock bottom, you may still utilize this horrible experience as an incentive to reach your financial goals. Every financial setback should be viewed as a teaching moment, and you should strive to navigate your ship toward and above your goals.

Examining and modifying your financial strategy

It is particularly challenging for those who subscribe to the concept of living paycheck to paycheck with little or no savings. While most individuals want to be financially independent, few people realize the importance of saving and investing until they are faced with a challenging circumstance. By having a plan in place and making frequent adjustments, you may advance toward reaching financial security.

You should take care of the following to ensure your financial security in the future:

1. Start by revising your objectives.

Your yearly financial planning process begins with establishing a goal that you are working to achieve. Prioritize your short-term and long-term objectives. These can include a desire to have children, take a trip, or retire early. Your tastes will unavoidably evolve over time. Consider these adjustments while formulating a new plan.

Knowing your goals and figuring out how to get there are the next two steps. Make sure your revenue is in line with the objectives you have set for yourself. You might need to make some tough choices, including reducing your monthly spending or paying off debt, if you find that your income isn't enough to support your necessities.

2. Monitor your cash flow.

The next action is to review your finances. It's essential to know how much money you make and how much money you spend in order to estimate your monthly cash flow. You may begin by calculating how much you spend on things like food, entertainment, power, and, among other things, your children's education.

Making a monthly budget for yourself is the next step. This will make it feasible for you to cut back on your non-essential spending and preserve money for your goals. Sometimes even $5 or $10 banknotes might be missed. However, you can avoid mistakes and keep control of your spending if you have a strategy in place for reviewing your budget.

3. Recognize the value of time.

Inflation is one of the primary reasons that lowers the value of money. Price hikes may limit your ability to buy some commodities in the future. Therefore, it is advisable to prepare for your goals within the constraints of time. Prices for goods and services will undoubtedly rise during the coming years. A house that costs $200,000 now can end up costing $400,000 in a few years. As a result, always account for inflation while setting goals.

Investing in retirement accounts, stocks, bonds, and shares is a smart way to combat growing prices. Being able to compound your money in addition to conserving it makes this vital. Getting a head start has advantages as well.

If you invest when you are in your 20s, the maturity advantage you would obtain after 30-40 years will be substantially bigger than if you buy when you are in your 30s or 40s. Early savers learn money management skills and are less likely to get into financial problems later in life.

4. Try to build a diverse portfolio.

Once you start investing, it is challenging to watch your money increase one day and decrease the next. The volatility can be greater if all of your assets are in a single asset class. In a volatile market, you can withdraw your money and risk suffering substantial losses.

It is better to keep your portfolio diversified with stocks, bonds, precious metals, real estate, and other assets that fit your risk tolerance. Every investor wants to reduce these risks, so you can use the financial advisor directory to find a financial advisor that can help you create a well-diversified portfolio.

5. Pay your Equated Monthly Instalments on time (EMIs)

Any financial obligations you presently have or plan to take on in the future must be understood. It is difficult to start down a secure financial path when you have debt. As a general rule, make an effort to finish repaying your debts before retiring. Having patience can also help you if you need to make budget cuts elsewhere.

A yearly review of your financial planning might help you cut back on credit card usage or check other loan repayments. Making a strategy at the outset will assist you in paying off your debt over time.

6. Consider your family.

If you are the sole provider, you might have to look after your loved ones, such as your husband or children. As a result, comprehensive financial planning calls for safeguards like insurance. Plans for life and health insurance can provide you with the assistance and funds you require to get through trying times. Making an estate plan is also essential. If you have a will that can ensure this, your goods will pass to their rightful heirs. You could also consider creating a trust if you have small children or kids with special needs.

7. Select the Ideal Retirement Date.

Different people may have different retirement objectives. A retiree who wants to downsize from a larger home might have different financial demands than a retiree who wants to upsize. Estimating the amount of money you'll need for retirement expenses in both situations is essential.

It could be helpful to start by listing your present expenses for things like food, housing, and leisure activities. When planning your retirement budget, it's critical to take your health and life insurance costs into account. Inflation will also need to be taken into consideration.

It will take at least 30 to 40 years to accumulate assets. As long as you have enough time, you may concentrate on your immediate objectives, such as purchasing a car or taking a dream vacation. Without making any extra cuts to your expenditure, you may balance your savings and current obligations.

For those who want to retire in their 40s, the "FIRE" movement advocates for early retirement and financial independence. To achieve this goal, you might need to save 50% of your yearly income. The FIRE concept's two pillars are boosting your income and cutting back on expenses.

Coping with setbacks and unexpected events

A career may not always go in a straight line. You could occasionally detect a reversal or a sense of immobility. Learn how to overcome obstacles to keep making progress. Everybody deals with problems in both their personal and professional lives. Those who desire to advance in their jobs do not let these issues deter them.

When facing obstacles, keep in mind the following traits and dispositions.

Realize your discomfort

Learning something new requires practice, much like becoming proficient at a new sport or musical instrument. Getting a new job or starting school are examples of this. You'll first experience some discomfort. That is the norm.

Many people lack confidence in unfamiliar circumstances. But act as though you are informed and a member of the team by acting that way. Never give up or return to your old behaviors. You'll gradually begin to feel more secure and at ease.

Always Try to Be Positive

Have confidence in yourself in all you do. You should plan on working hard at work. Employers and coworkers like those with a "can-do" attitude.

Try out new endeavors and talents. You'll err from time to time. You'll also have a lot of success. Consider the benefits or lessons you took away from each unexpected experience. Utilize the knowledge you have gained to improve your work. You can overcome obstacles if you have an optimistic outlook.

Be responsible

When things aren't going well, it's simple to pass the responsibility to someone else. However, if you are unwilling to acknowledge your contribution to the problem, you will not be able to resolve it. At work, judgments are occasionally made, or you can find yourself in situations that are beyond your control. One can be impartial. Don't let it disturb you. You have control over how you respond in difficult circumstances.

Adapt to constructive criticism

It's normal for a superior or colleague with greater experience to provide you with comments. You can complete your tasks more successfully as a result. It doesn't imply that the speaker holds a negative opinion of you in particular. Maintain your composure, pay close attention, and consider how their suggestions can improve your productivity at work.

Ask Questions and Form Relationships

Find out who can answer your inquiries when you are unfamiliar with a situation. You will then learn about the expectations for your role in terms of behavior. For instance, coworkers could explain your responsibilities. The rules are accessible to your employer.

Find coworkers you enjoy working with, and help one another out by sharing knowledge and providing answers to one another's inquiries. Collaboration for shared professional objectives You and your partner should talk to them about any workplace issues that worry you. Do not be negative or whine. Your perspective will change as a result of the interaction. At the office, people will value you more.

Celebrating accomplishments and important dates

Major anniversaries should be commemorated for more than simply births, weddings, and graduations. A milestone may be of any size or shape. They might be anything, including finishing a challenging task at work, performing well on an exam, or making a sizable home improvement. In today's fast-paced society, people usually forget to congratulate or thank themselves since they are focused on starting the next task right away.

Personal development is crucial. Whether you've learned a new skill, landed a new job, or aced a class, rewarding yourself for your accomplishments may motivate you to take the next step. Why? Because achieving smaller goals will inspire you to accomplish bigger ones.

If one of your goals is to learn a new language, for instance, be sure to congratulate yourself when you meet your daily or weekly study goals. Weekly appreciation may entail treating yourself to lunch at your preferred restaurant, while daily celebrations could be as simple as indulging in a piece of your favorite chocolate.

Celebrating successes encourages constructive attitudes and behaviors, both of which are necessary when tackling a new task or difficulty. Remembering milestones may motivate you to accomplish future successes, whether you're celebrating with coworkers after your team won a significant client, with classmates after passing a challenging semester, or with your spouse after surviving the first few weeks of being a new parent.

CHAPTER 7

CONCLUSION

The significance of lifelong learning and development

"Continuous learning" refers to the ongoing expansion of knowledge and skill sets. Continuous learning at work, which is typically used in the context of professional development, is about developing new skills and information while also solidifying what has already been learned.

Daily rituals and practices are the foundation of continuous learning. For continuous learning, any form of ongoing knowledge intake can be applied. It might be finished in a specific period of time or continue all throughout one's life.

The notion of "continuous learning" is broad and can be formal or informal, organized or unstructured. Studying, conversing casually, using a skill in practice, seeking assistance with a new topic, observing more experienced employees, enrolling in a formal course, and observing them are a few examples of activities.

Components of lifelong learning

Maintaining knowledge and skills throughout time is the aim of continuous learning in the workplace. Conventional training techniques state that after a single intense training session, employee knowledge often reaches a peak before gradually slipping away over time owing to a lack of reinforcement.

Knowledge among employees is the result of various learning occasions in continuous learning. Continuous learning, which is sustained by regular practice sessions, may help a company raise staff knowledge levels.

Beyond material wealth, living a full life

Do you feel dissatisfied when you pursue wealth? Do you experience anxiety or even depression at the thought of always seeking more money? Do you find it profoundly unsatisfactory to think that your worth is determined by your wealth?

12 Infinitely Valuable Items for a Wealthy Life

1. Reliability

Knowing who you are and always being loyal to who you are is the greatest wealth in life. Every morning, tell yourself in the mirror that being true to yourself will be your greatest service. Regardless of my financial situation or lack of "status," I feel content just doing this. At the beginning of your Riches in My Life diary, identify yourself as the sincere, spiritually wealthy person that you are.

2. Acceptance

In order for acceptance and tranquility to replace your fundamental need to control life's uncontrollable events, you must overcome this urge. Every time you catch yourself wishing you could change the unchangeable, note it in your journal and reassure yourself, "It's okay." The current state of affairs is favorable.

3. Curiousness

You still feel awed in a childlike way. A rich mind is one that experiments and queries all the time. When I learn something new, no matter how minor, that I can't wait to share with others, those are always my favorite days.

To renew your zest for life, read a variety of genres, learn about foreign cultures, and go deeper into anything that fascinates you. You'll be astounded if you record these novel discoveries in your True Riches diary.

4. Originality

A bold act that produces a valuable quality—kindness, according to Confucius—that can be observed in spiritual leaders like Gandhi and Buddha—is creating something out of nothing. Strongness without abruptness or unpleasantness is a crucial and unusual quality. Next time the kids or a coworker act inappropriately, smile, use kind words, and document your response in your diary.

5. Resilience

It might be challenging to cultivate patience in today's world of instant gratification. However, if you are persistent, you may finally achieve goals that at first seem insurmountable. I used to exclaim, "Missy, I need it now or never," but writing has let me experience the joy that bigger, longer-term projects provide. Make a realistic timeline in your diary and remind yourself to be patient with yourself the next time you catch yourself berating yourself for not accomplishing a goal.

6. Gratitude It takes dedication to evaluate your belongings and show gratitude. But taking note of all the good things in life will make you content and successful. Set a goal for yourself to add one thing to your diary each day that you may have taken for granted in order to build a treasury of blessings.

7. Kindness

When you give when you believe you can't offer enough of yourself, you are truly being generous. You realize that you always have much to share as a result of this. Give someone your undivided attention for 30 minutes when you feel you don't have time. One of the kindest things you can do in today's hectic culture is to provide your undivided attention. Make a note of these acts of kindness in your diary.

8. Generosity

Being kind offers many advantages of its own, such as inner peace, satisfaction, and the knowledge that you are actually making a difference in the world that others will remember. The next time you are unhappy or critical of yourself, first perform a small act of kindness for someone else. Discuss them in your journal.

9. Kindness

True selflessness is the ability to recognize and empathize with another person's pain. The areas of ease and plenty in your own life are visible to you. In your notebook, note all of your kind thoughts and acts. I believe that these writings are the most powerful ones in my diary because every time I read them again, they give me the feeling of being covered in blessings.

10. Love

Emotionally-based relationships, whether they be with a spouse, a family member, or a friend, provide you with a wealth that no amount of money could ever hope to match. Every day, express your affection to someone, and in your diary, jot down the kind things they say to you.

11. Susceptibility

When you let down your guard and expose your weaknesses, other people are better able to see the entire picture rather than just a silhouette. Vulnerability serves as the cornerstone of relationships. This is my weakness, yet by purposefully letting people in, casual encounters have blossomed into beautiful friendships. Write down all the times in your notebook when you felt brave and vulnerable to help you form this rewarding habit.

12. Satisfaction

Realizing that you have abundance in your life brings you peace and satisfaction. To be able to do this in a world of materialism takes a special gift. Check your notebook for all the unimaginably precious possessions you don't have. Recognize your current luck since "enough is a feast," as the saying goes.

www.ingramcontent.com/pod-product-compliance
Lightning Source LLC
Chambersburg PA
CBHW070313220526
45465CB00004B/1856